GW01564260

Lote Tree Learning

+1 832- 378-7365

hello@lotetreelearning.com

www.lotetreelearning.com

Ordering Information:

Quantity sales. Special discounts are available on quantity purchases by corporations, associations, and others. For details, contact us at the address above.

Printed in the United States of America

First Edition

Illustrations by Israa Alaa Ismail

Lote Tree
LEARNING

ANCILENTS

History
Connections
Book 1
Middle Grades

MAPS & RUBRICS

SUMAIA B. MICHEL, DRS
SARA MAGDY

Lote Tree
LEARNING

LOCATION MAPS

Map of Greece

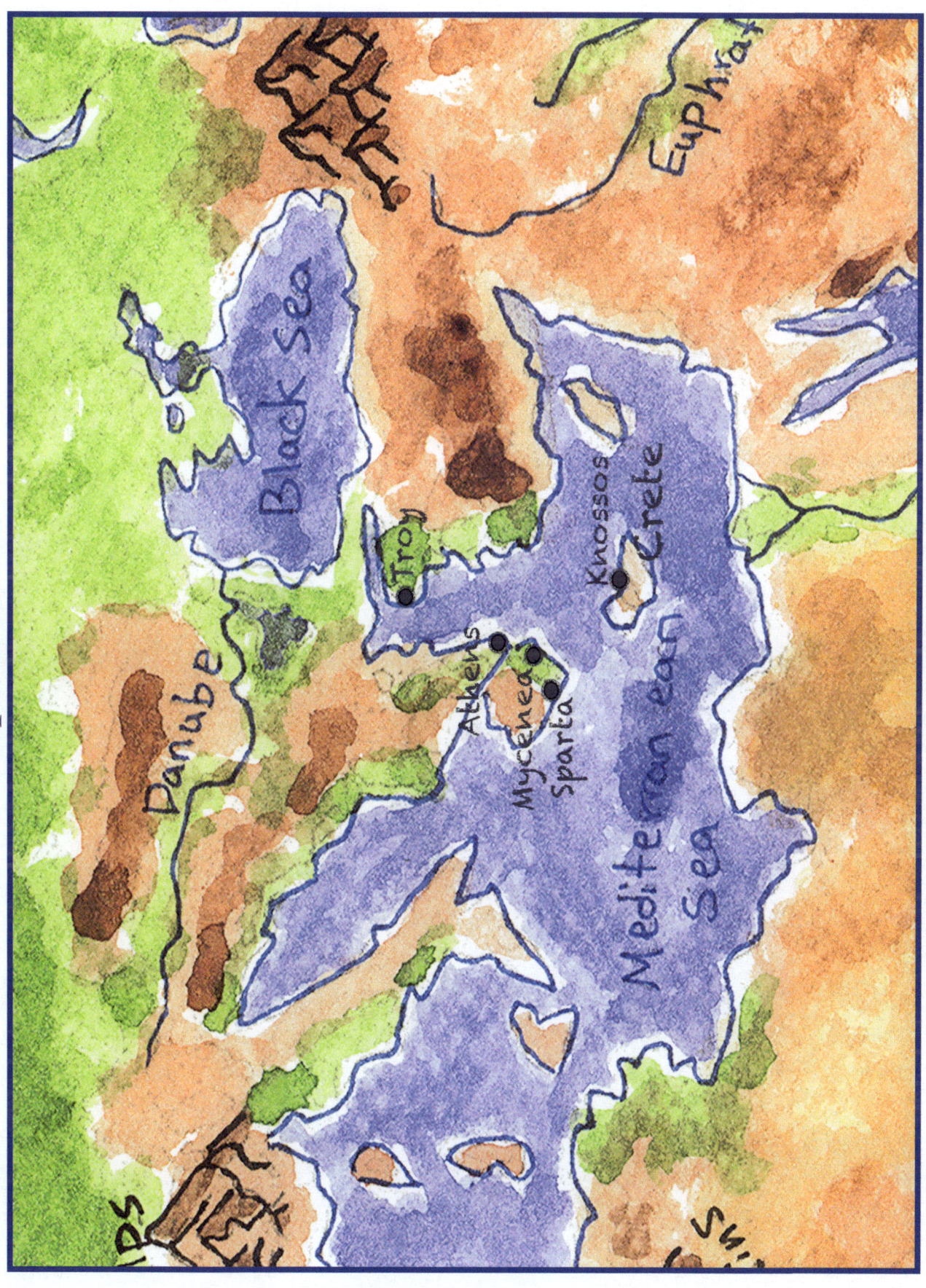

Euphrates

Black Sea

Danube

Troy

Knossos

Crete

Athens

Mycenea

Sparta

Mediterranean Sea

Map of Mesopotamia & Arabia

Indus

Arabian Sea

Caspian

Zagros

Tigris

Euphrates

Black Sea

Hattushash

Harran

Nineveh

Babylon

Ur

Aleppo

Damascus

Nazareth

Byblos

Jaffa

Jerusalem

Bethlehem

Hebron

Petra

Soddom

Eilat

Madyan

Mekkah

Ahqaf

Hadramut

Sana'a

Yemen

Aden

Cairo

Nile

an ean

Map of Creation

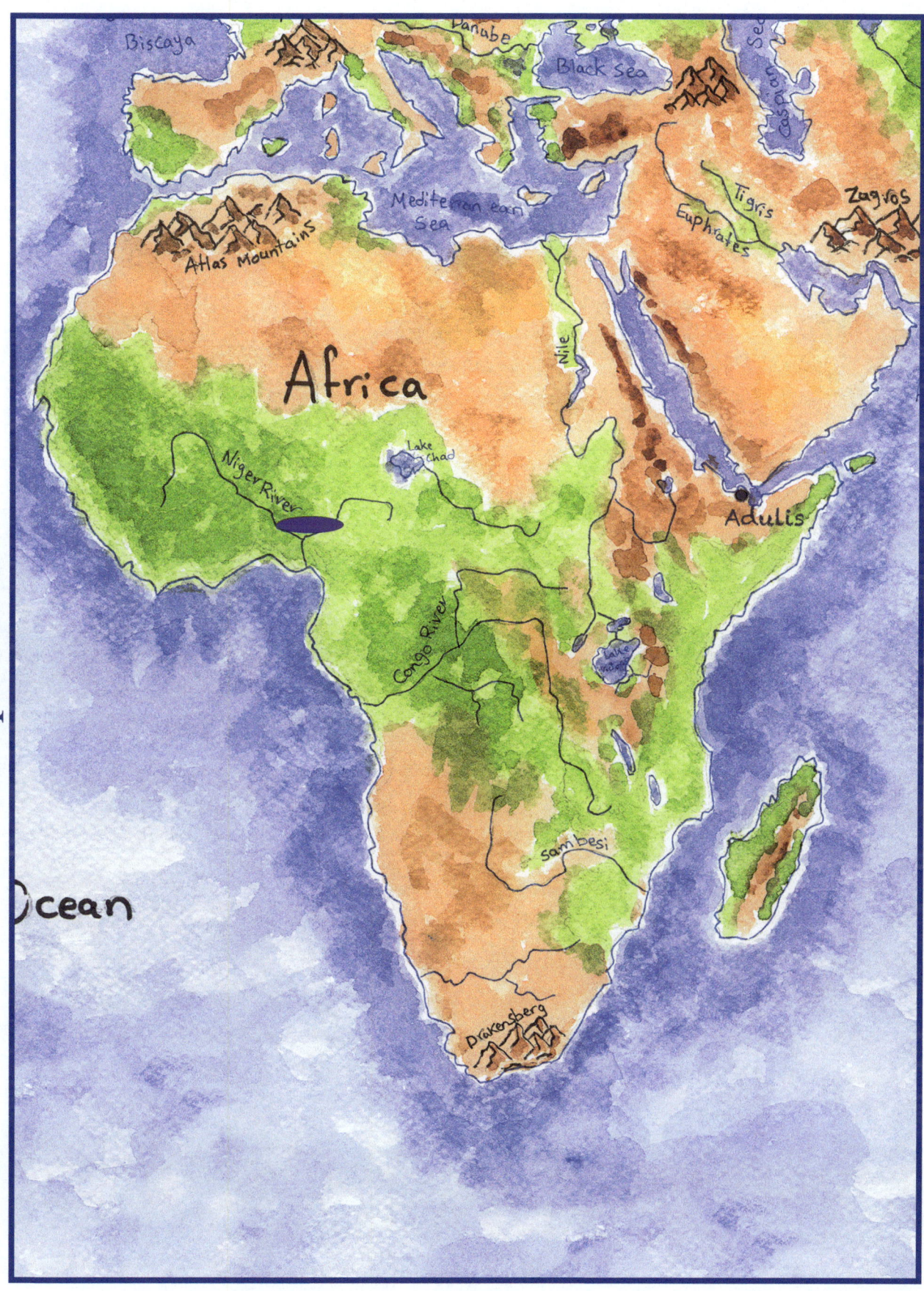

Map of Africa

Map of Americas

Map of Asia

Asia

Yellow River

Yangtze

Mekong

South China Sea

Bay of Bengal

Ganges

Himalaya

Indus

Zagros

Arabian Sea

Map of China

Map of Eurasia

Indus

Arabian Sea

Zagros

Persepolis

Caspian Sea

Babylon Tigris

Euphrates

Black Sea

Nile

Danube

Athens
Sparta

Mediterranean Sea

Map of Europe

Volga

Europe

Caspian Sea

Tigris

Euphrates

Black Sea

Danube

Hallstatt

Alps

Rome

Mediterranean Sea

Carthage

Atlas Mountains

North Sea

Gulf of Biscaya

Map of Nile Delta

Mediterranean Sea

Euphrates

Nile

Lake Chad

Map of Mediterranean Area

WORLD WALL MAP

Fully assembled, the World Wall Map should look like this:

TREE TRUNK TIMELINE

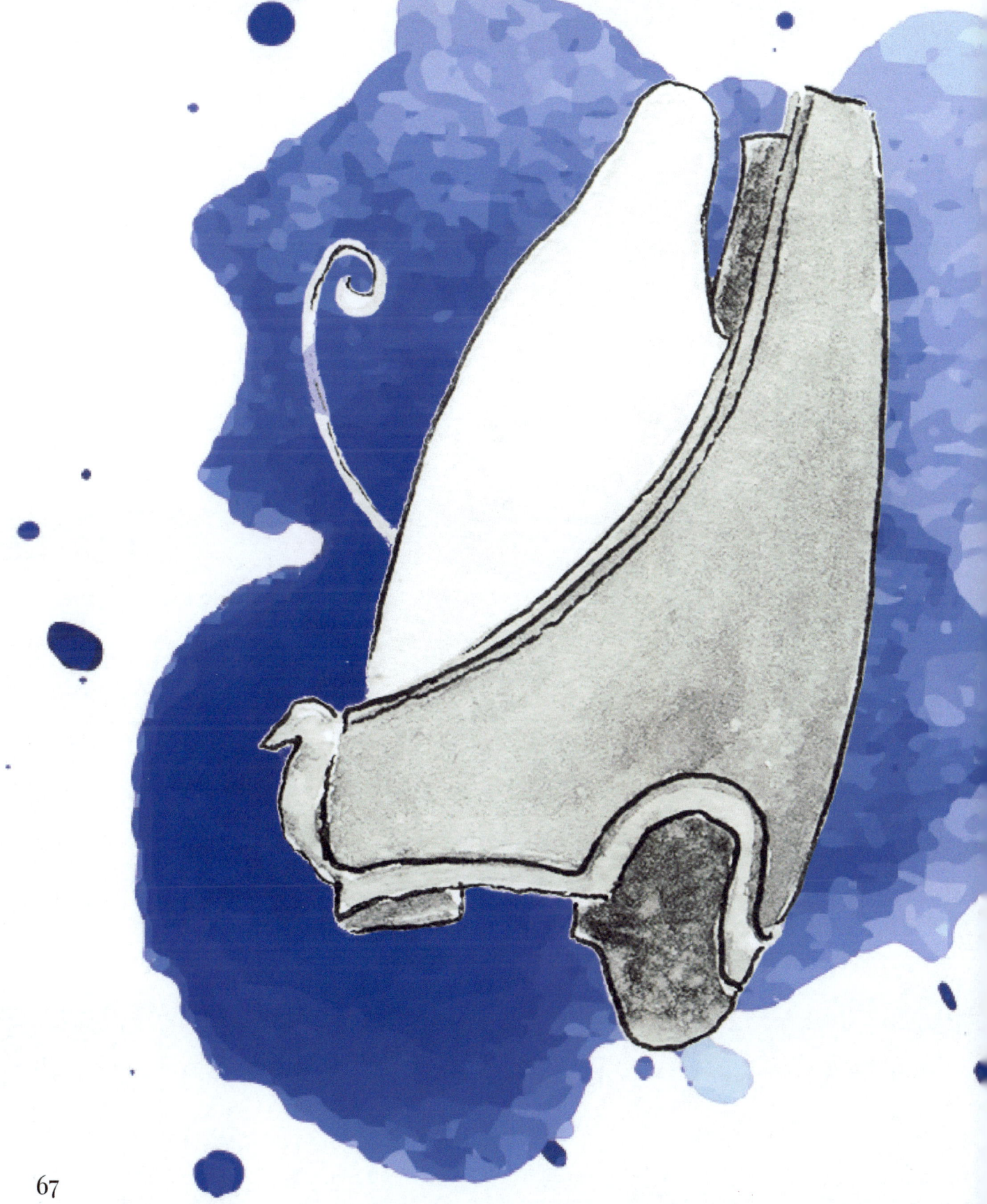

Fully assembled, the Tree Trunk Timeline should
look like this:

TREE TRUNK TIMELINE

TREE TRUN

Arabia

K TIMELINE

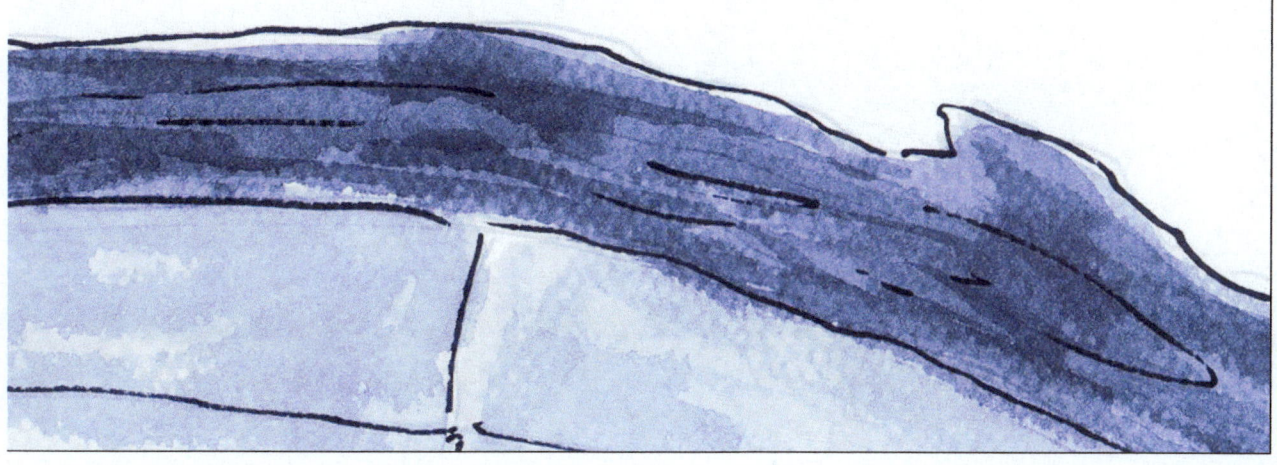

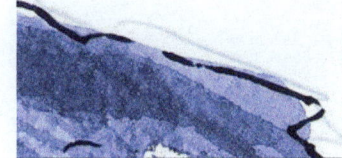

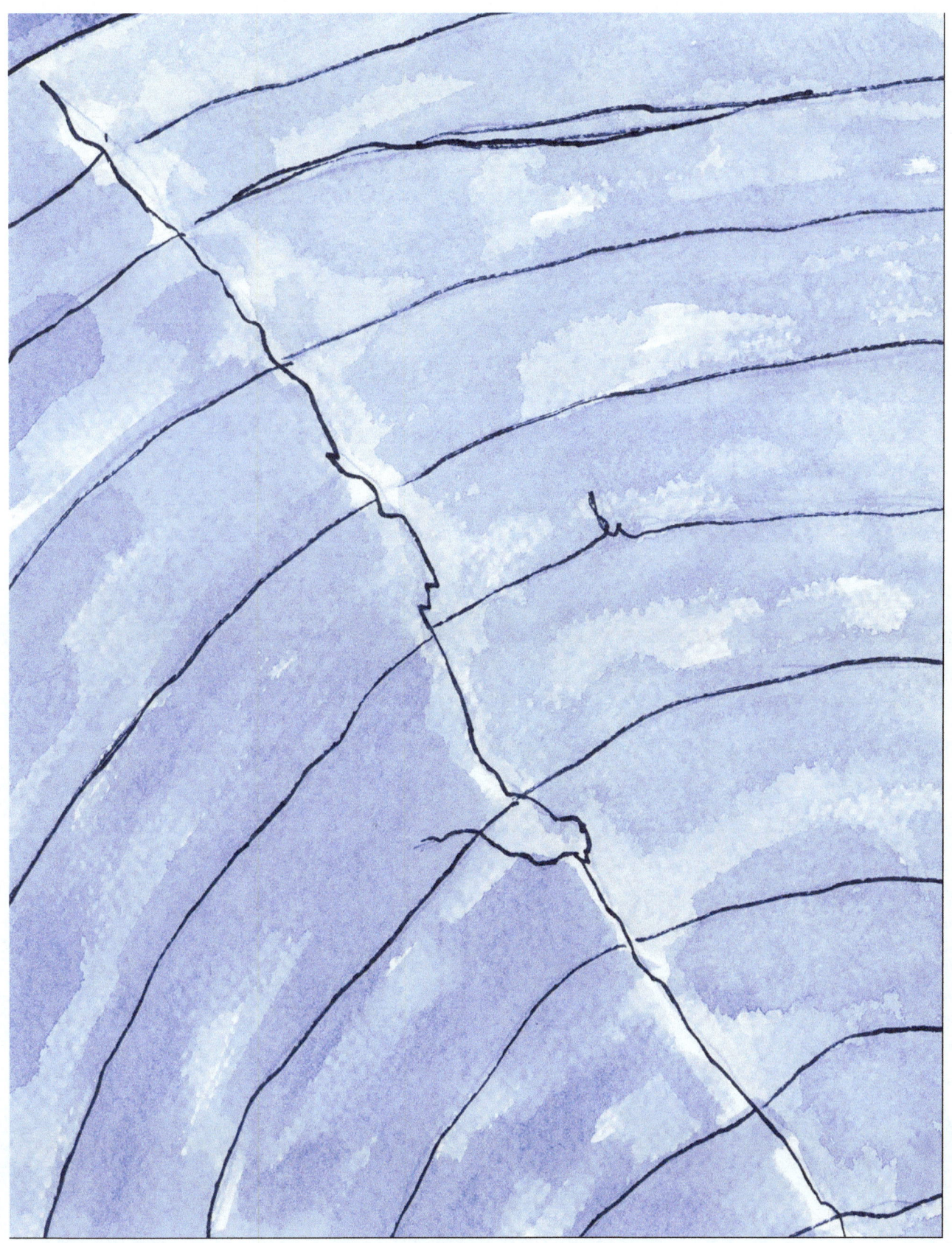

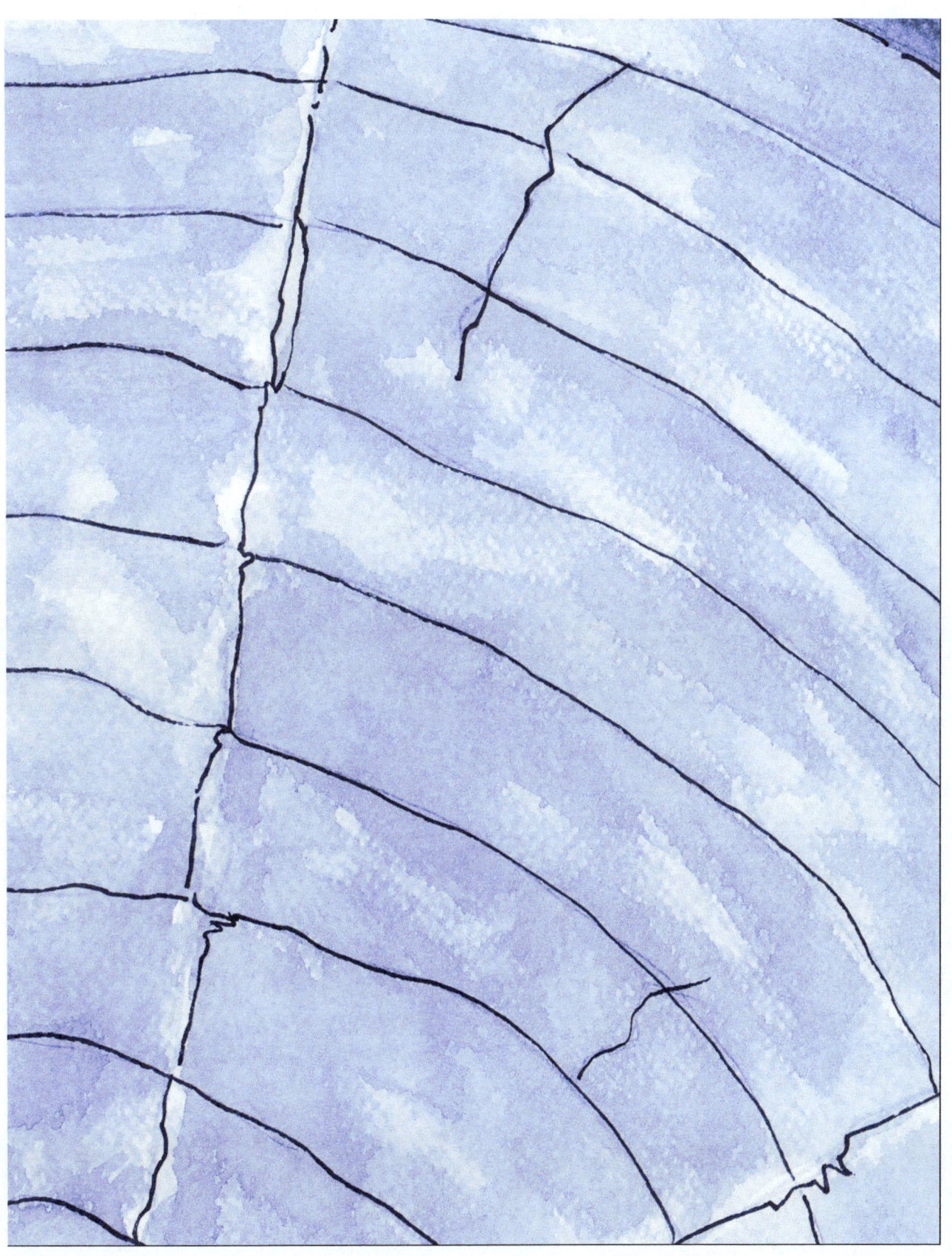

Dates

0 CE – 500 AD

500 BCE – 0 CE

1000–500 BCE

1500–1000 BCE

2000–1500 BCE

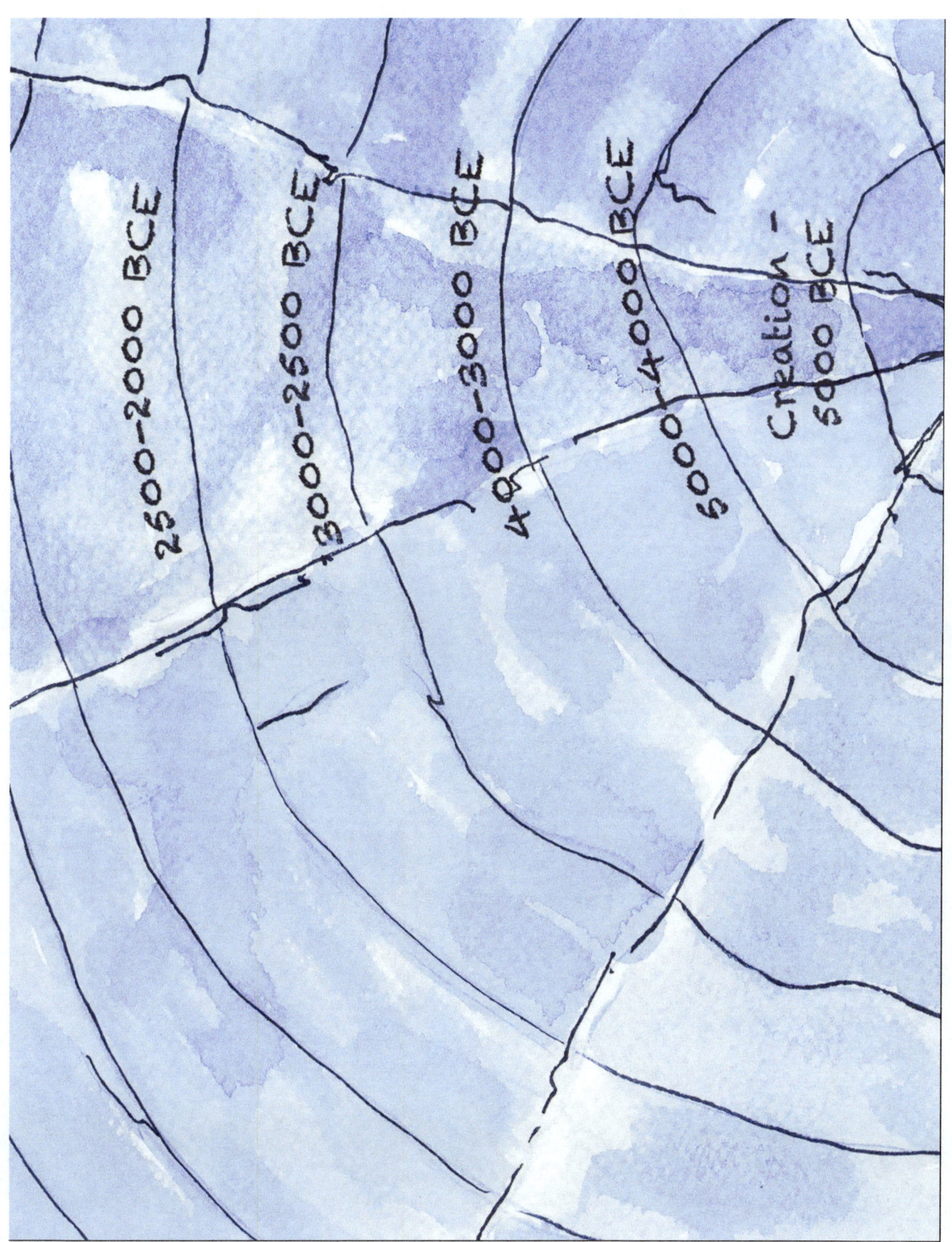

2500–2000 BCE

3000–2500 BCE

4,000–3000 BCE

5000–4000 BCE

Creation – 5000 BCE

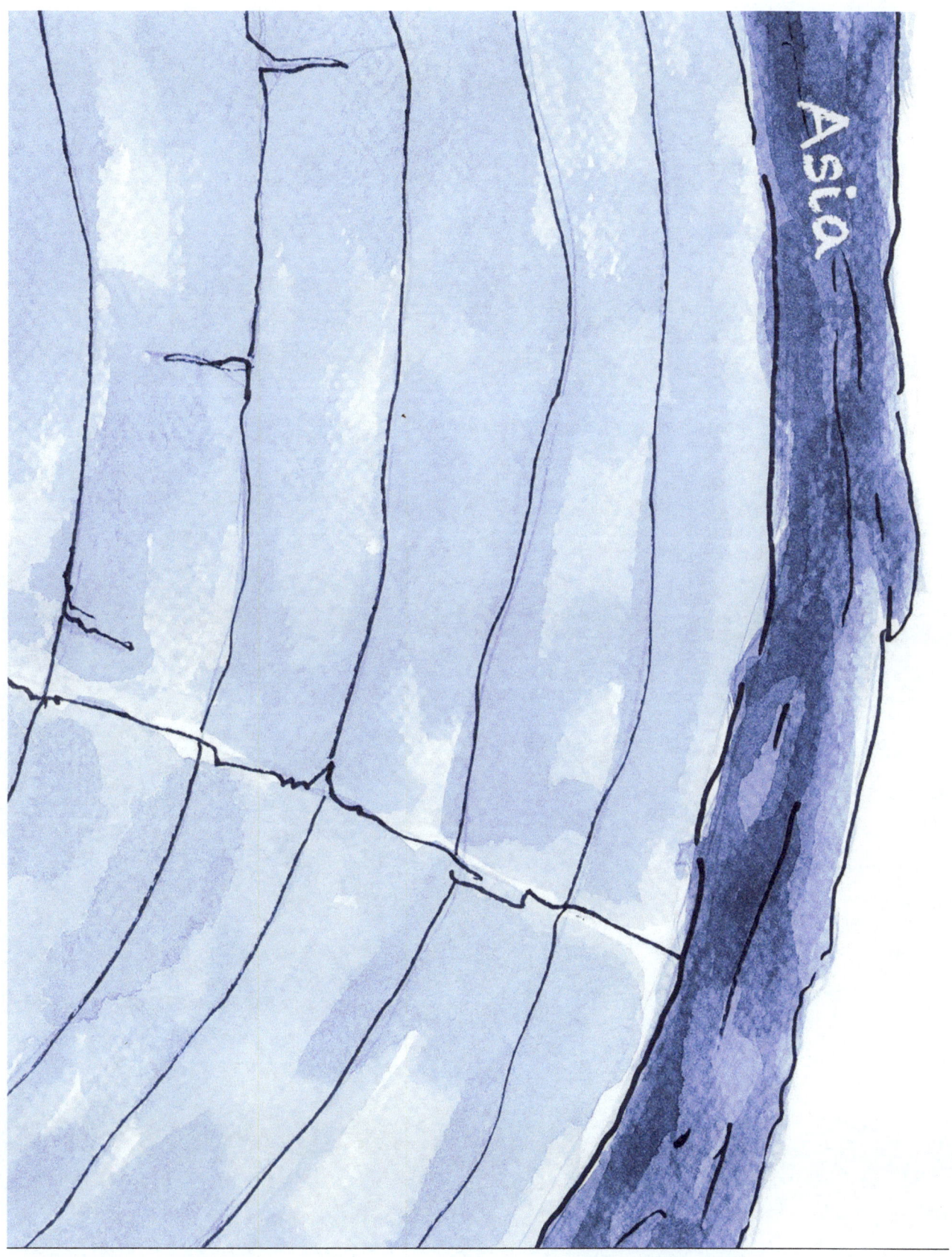

Asia

93

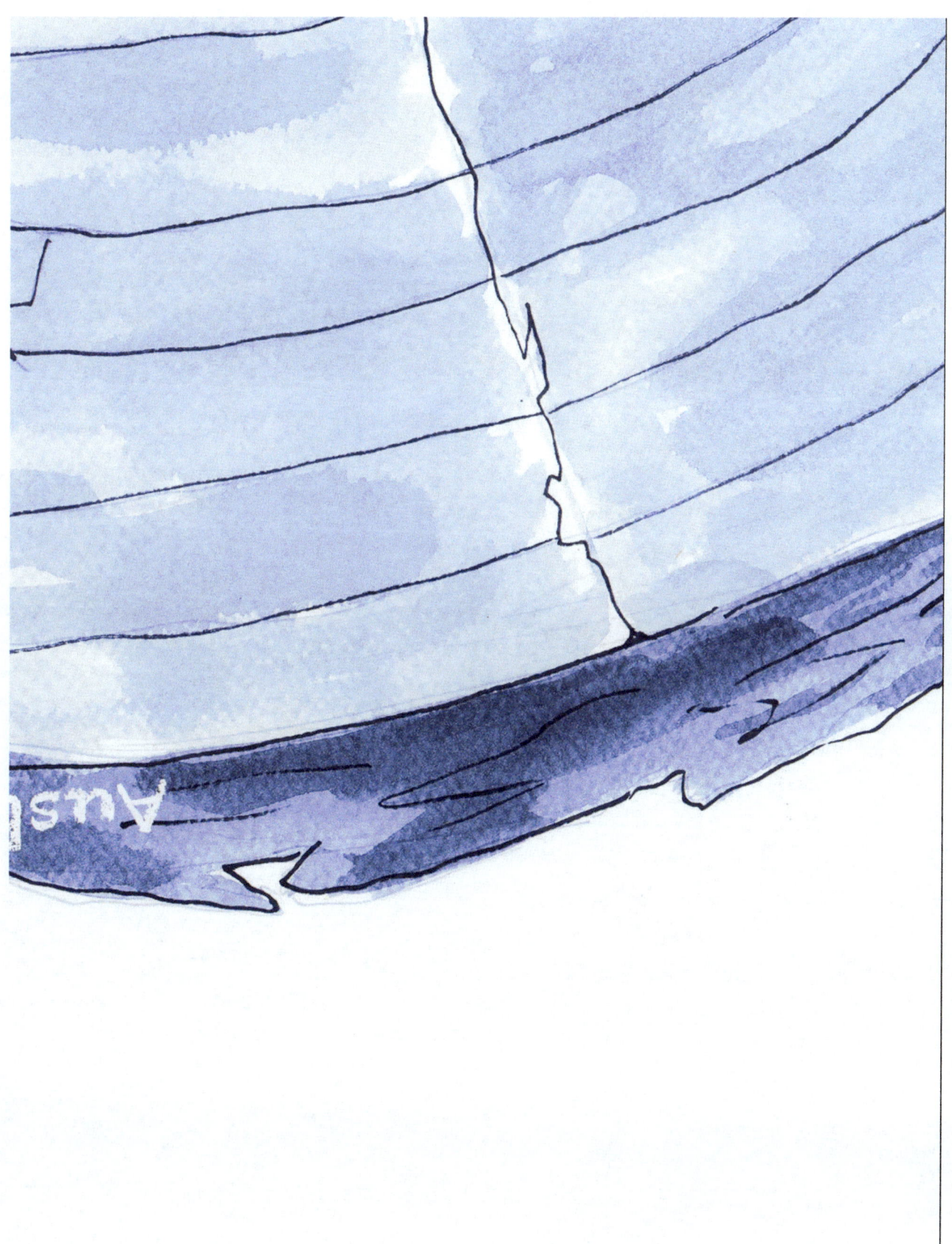

RUBRICS & CHECK-LISTS

RUBRICS

Rubric Poster

	Awesome!	Cool	Nah...	What?!
The title & Subtitle	Topic and title clear and easily identified. Main idea is clearly appropriate to topic.	Topic and title are mostly clear and easily identified Main idea is appropriate to topic	Topic and title difficult to identify Main idea not clearly stated	Topic and title are not clearly identified No main idea
Graphics	All illustrations complement purpose of visual All Illustrations are of the same theme/color All illustrations are of high quality	Most illustrations complement purpose of visual Most Illustrations are of the same theme/color Most illustrations are of high quality	Few illustrations complement purpose of visual Few Illustrations are of the same theme/color Few illustrations are of high quality	Illustrations do not complement purpose of visual Illustrations are of different theme/color Illustrations are of low quality
Lay-out & White Space	Outstanding use of design and space Original and creative design Overall design is pleasing and harmonious	Adequate use of design and space Design is adequate Overall design is mostly pleasing and harmonious	Inappropriate use of design and space Design lacks creativity Lack of harmonious design in presentation	Little attempt to use design and space appropriately Design is dull Project has sloppy appearance
Colors	Outstanding use of color, Colors are complementary Colors are used to highlight important points	Adequate use of color Colors are complementary Color do not highlight important points	Inappropriate use of color Colors are low-contrast Colors highlight important points	Little attempt to use color Colors are low contrast and make reading difficult. Colors are not used to highlight important points

Rubric Diagramming

	Awesome!	Cool	Nah...	What?!
Information	The problem is clearly presented in the diagram: within one glance the problem becomes clear	The problem is adequately presented in the diagram	The problem is unclearly presented in the diagram: only with verbal explanation does the problem become clear	The problem is not at all presented in the diagram
Diagram	The diagram chosen reflects the problem and the relationship of its components	The diagram chosen reflects the problem but not clearly the relationship of its components	The diagram chosen reflects the problem but not the relationship of its components	The diagram chosen does not reflect the problem
Colors	Several complementary colors are used to highlight the elements of the diagram	Several colors are used but they are not complementary Colors are used to highlight the elements of the diagram	Few colors are used but they are not complementary Colors are not used to highlight the elements of the diagram	No colors are used
Mechanics labeling	The diagram is labeled correctly The elements are labeled as well.	The diagram is labeled correctly But the elements are not labeled.	The diagram is not labeled correctly	The diagram is not labeled

Rubric PowerPoint

	Awesome!	Cool	Nah...	What?!
Quantity	More than 7 slides Intro and conclusion slides present	Slides are adequate to present topic Intro and conclusion slides present	Slides sufficient to present topic No intro and conclusion slides present	Too little slides to present topic No intro and conclusion slides present
Template	Template lay-out is suitable for the topic Title is catchy Colors are adjusted	Template lay-out is suitable for the topic Title is present but not catchy Colors are adjusted	Template lay-out is not suitable for the topic or colors are not adjusted Or fields are left blank (if made online)	No lay-out templates used
Graphs	Graphs are two or more and are informative Colors are aligned to the design	Graphs are informative, but very few Colors are not aligned to the design	Graphs are used but not informative	No graphs used
Slide design	One main point per slide Colors are supportive of the topic	One main point per slide Colors are not supportive of the topic or distract	Too much information per slide	Too much or no info on the slides
Graphics & Images	Support the main topic All illustrations are aligned to each other	Support the main topic Illustrations are not aligned to each other	Do not support the main topic	No graphics or images used

Rubric Mind Map

	Awesome!	Cool	Nah...	What?!
preparation	One main idea per sticky note Grouped into clusters	Too much info on sticky notes Grouped into clusters	Used sticky notes Not grouped into clusters	Did not use sticky notes
Central idea	One clear central idea that clearly relates to the topic	One clear central idea that does not clearly relates to the topic	One central idea but did not relate to topic	No central idea
Branches	Uses main branches and several sub branches. Uses tertiary branches	Uses main branches and several sub branches.	Uses main branches and no sub branches	No main branches
Keywords/links	Use keywords on the main branches and the subbranches. Uses links between different subbranches	Use keywords on the main branches and the subbranches.	Uses keywords on the main branches only	Uses no keywords
Colors & graphics	Uses colors for each main branch and its subbranches Uses images/drawings	Uses colors for each main branch and its subbranches	Uses colors for each main branch	Does not use colors or images

CHECK-LISTS

Check-list Outlining

Uses one main point per line

Uses Roman Numerals

Uses on phrase per Roman Numeral

Uses secondary points

Uses lower case letters for secondary points

Check-list Note Taking

Writes definitions

Uses own words

Uses number list and/or bullet points

Uses abbreviations

Check-list Summarizing

Uses own words

Reduces every paragraph to one or two sentences